THAILAND

"*Give us this day our daily rice*": novitiates receive alms early in the morning, though they fast till midday.

THAILAND

by DEREK A. C. DAVIES

 KODANSHA INTERNATIONAL LTD.
TOKYO, NEW YORK & SAN FRANCISCO

Distributed in the United States by Kodansha International/USA Ltd., through Harper & Row, Publishers, Inc., 10 East 53rd Street, New York, New York 10022.

Published by Kodansha International Ltd., 12-21, Otowa 2-chome, Bunkyo-ku, Tokyo 112 and Kodansha International/ USA Ltd., 10 East 53rd Street, New York, New York 10022 and 44 Montgomery Street, San Francisco, California 94104.
LCC 72-100627
ISBN 0-87011-116-7
JBC 0326-789527(0)-2361

First edition, 1970
Fifth printing, 1981

Contents

ACKNOWLEDGEMENTS

I am most grateful to Miss Panngham Boriraj for her help in making arrangements to take some of the pictures and to my wife Sumiko for her cooperation.

All photographs were taken by the author except plates 19, 20, 34, 36, 38, which were taken by J. Farrell, and the front jacket photo by Bernard Sonneville. Line drawings by Sumiko Davies.

NOTE ON THE TEXT

Transliteration of Thai is made difficult by the fact that it is a tonal language, and even in Thailand there are many different ways of romanization. In general, I have followed common English pronunciation; however, in names of places, the older systems have been adopted for so long that it would be unnatural to change them. Thus in "ph," "dh," and "th," the "h" is silent; the word "Thai" itself would, by pronunciation, be more natural as "Tai," but custom has resulted in the former being adopted.

Bangkok

City of Angels

It was March 22, 1966, when I first arrived in Bangkok—and it was, coincidentally, my twenty-third birthday. I wanted to see something of the world and six months before, after graduating from college in England, I had crossed Russia by the trans-Siberian railway for Japan. Now, after a brief stop in Hongkong, I found myself leaning on the railing of the *Vietnam* (a Messagerie Maritime ship) as she nosed her way slowly up the Chao Phya River from the Gulf of Siam to Bangkok. I stood at the railing and watched the thick carpet of jungle that stretched out flat from either bank turn from deep green to purple in the glow of the setting sun.

I had no idea, as we headed through the jungle toward the capital, how long I would be staying in Thailand. A month, perhaps? Two? Three? Certainly my first twilit glimpse of that lovely country made me feel I wanted to stay as long as I could—and there is, to me, something particularly adventurous about landing in a strange country with no special plans to stay and yet with no fixed date to leave either. How long I remained in Thailand would depend on how well I liked living there. As things turned out, I left, with great reluctance, a year and a half later.

In a village by the river, the curling, golden roof of a temple, reflecting the last rays of the setting sun, was glinting like a rare jewel against the purple velvet of the jungle beyond. A small canoe, paddled by a market woman whose skin was as dark as the teak that came from the forests of the north, bobbed precariously in our wake, looking as though it might capsize at any moment. But she was obviously an experienced oarswoman, and her little canoe came to no harm. Young boys, taking their evening swim, waved at us as we glided by, a giant white phantom in the fading light.

On the dock, after landing, I hired a three-wheeled taxi (known in Bangkok as a *samlor*), and, with my suitcases beside me, bumped and rattled my way toward Chinatown, where I had been told about an inexpensive hotel. (Bangkok's grand new Western-style hotels are no cheaper than their counterparts elsewhere in the world.)

Some cities—Venice, for instance—make an immediate and permanent impression on the traveler as he first enters; with other cities, particularly where one has to cross large, often shoddy, suburbs before reaching the city's heart, first impressions are meaningless. Entering Bangkok from the port, one finds this to be particularly true, for the road to the center is quite without character. Three- or four-story white concrete buildings, with a shop on the ground floor and offices and apartments above, stand next to vacant lots growing wild with exuberant tropical vegetation, while at the same time the grand houses of the well-to-do rub shoulders with the more modest houses, standing on stilts, of poorer folk and with clusters of tin-roofed shacks that almost certainly belong to squatters.

Other first impressions, as we swayed along toward Chinatown: there seem to be more Japanese cars than those of any other country on the streets of Bangkok—and more Japanese motorcycles than there are in Tokyo. Thailand, being flat and always warm, is ideally suited to two-wheeled travel. (That particular first impression turned out to be an accurate one: as I was to discover later, Japan is Thailand's biggest trading partner.)

And the people? Most of the men I saw, it seemed to me, were wearing simple shirts and trousers and no tie, but the dress of the women offered considerably more variety. Many of the older women wore what I was to learn later was the native costume: a white blouse and a long, densely patterned kind of skirt that reached all the way down to the ankles (called, as I was to learn, a *pasin*); younger women seemed to prefer either tight pants or Western-style summer dresses in bright Thai silks and cottons. Many Chinese women wore baggy, black pajama trousers beneath a white blouse. I also saw Indian Sikhs with their white turbans and saffron-robed Buddhist monks. Most of the little children playing beside the road were wholly or almost wholly naked.

Suddenly I caught my breath. Although we were now in a highly congested area, with cars, motorcycles, and people milling about, the driver of the *samlor* took his hands off the wheel in order to execute a little boxing mime. He looked at me with a smile and nodded toward a large building that was obviously a sports stadium. I understood that he was telling me I might see Thai kick-boxing there, and I smiled—somewhat weakly—back. I began to breathe again only after the driver put his hands back on the wheel.

Yet only a few moments later they were off again: we were passing a temple, and the driver's hands were pressed reverently together, palm to palm. It was my first indication of the important role Buddhism plays in Thai life, and I decided that we were less likely to have an accident if the driver was praying than if he was

THAILAND ✳

boxing—or perhaps I was merely getting used to his "Look, Ma, no hands" attitude. (Later, driving about the country, I was to see almost all the passengers in a bus, as well as its driver, *wai* in this manner—just as in many countries Catholics cross themselves when they pass a church.)

In any case, I was much relieved when we drew up in front of my hotel—the Thai Song Greet—and I no longer had to pass judgment on the relative safety of praying or boxing when you are driving a *samlor* through the crowded streets of Bangkok. The entrance to the hotel was through the rather grimy kitchen of its restaurant. It was not the sort of entrance favored by Cesar Ritz, but then I had hardly expected it to be. I was conducted up the stairs at the back to my room, which was small and sparsely furnished, with a wide wooden bed covered in mosquito netting and a rather shaky dressing table. Overhead was a large fan, and on the stone floor beside the bed stood a tin spittoon.

It was very hot. Through the open window came the blare of the traffic outside. The fan did little more than listlessly stir the sluggish air. The bed was very hard, yet I lay back with a sigh of contentment, thankful that at least on my first day in Bangkok I had avoided death in its murderous traffic.

✳   ✳

Soon, almost as though the Buddha in his infinite compassion had decided to make me a gift of Thailand, I had a job, a house, a maid to look after me, and a motorbike to take me out into the country or to one or another of Thailand's many extremely beautiful beaches.

✻ BANGKOK—"CITY OF ANGELS"

The job first, of course: that was the fulcrum on which all the other amenities rested. I was hired to do some writing and photographing for the magazine section of the *Bangkok Post*, the city's largest English-language newspaper. It was pleasant and interesting work, and it had the further advantage of allowing me to travel about the country, thus discovering many things about Thailand that, as an ordinary tourist, I could never have known. Much of the material in this book is based on up-country trips I made while working for the *Post*.

Once I had my job, I rented a small wooden house of two stories, built in the native style, with wide, screened windows upstairs. Lying there my first night, looking out at the tender Southeast Asian sky, I felt almost as though I was sleeping under the stars. There was of course a little garden, for the Thais are very fond of their plots of green, with a tree or two and some flowers. In my garden there grew a coconut palm (though I never saw a nut on it), with a lush, brilliantly crimson bougainvillaea that made up for the palm tree's niggardliness. For all this splendor I paid less than a hundred American dollars a month.

And once I had the house, I soon found—rather to my surprise —that I also had a servant. I had not especially wanted one, but wages for domestic help are so low in Thailand that she came well within my budget—and she was, in addition, one of the kindest, gentlest old women I have ever known. So wizened and feeble-looking was she that I doubted at first whether she would be capable of doing any work (and I wondered, in fact, if it was opium that had brought her to that condition), but I quickly discovered that she was extremely hard-working and highly intelligent.

What's more, she was a first-class cook. It took me a little while

THAILAND ✻

to acquire a taste for Thai food, but once I did, I found it delicious
—hot and spicy to be sure, but with its own unique cuisine and
enormously varied. Almost any fruit or vegetable known to man will
grow in the rich, moist soil of Thailand, so a Thai cook always has
a plentifully stocked market around the corner to choose from. I
often breakfasted in my little garden, feasting on one or another of
the country's hundred or more varieties of fruit. Thai desserts I
found especially delicious: it was only after I left the country that
I realized how much I was going to miss them—and the many hot
and spicy dishes that preceded them.

Once I got accustomed to Bangkok's erratic traffic that had so
startled me on arrival (which did not, after all, take very long),
I bought a motorbike, a little Suzuki 125, and with it darted through
the congestion of the streets to see the sights of the capital and,
on weekends, to get out of the city to the country or the sea. Thailand has some of the most beautiful beaches in the world, a number
of fascinating villages, and a pleasant, easy-going people who are
always ready to welcome the stranger.

One of the first Thai words the foreigner learns is *snuk*, which
means "fun," or "entertainment," or "amusement." The Thais
are masters of *snuk*—and soon the foreigner, if he lives amongst
them for any time, learns to grow a little more relaxed too. But it
is doubtful, I fear, if any Westerner can ever be as relaxed and as
ready to laugh as a Thai. "*Mai penrai*," he says when something un-
pleasant happens: "Never mind." So said a Thai friend when I told
him I had lost my camera; then, seeing I remained unconsoled,
he pointed out that I might have lost all three of my cameras—or
even got myself killed in a traffic accident. He laughed as he said
this, and I soon found myself laughing with him. *Mai penrai*!

✳ BANGKOK—"CITY OF ANGELS"

Mostly flat and fertile, Thailand possesses a total area of about two hundred thousand square miles, nearly half of which is covered by some kind of forest. Forest land is to be found in every part of the country except the central plain. Looked at on the map, Thailand bears a remarkable resemblance to the head of an elephant, one of her most important animals and at one time one of her chief exports. She shares her borders with four other countries, Burma, Laos, Cambodia, and Malaysia; and her population of thirty-three million is made up of a wide variety of ethnic groups—though by far the largest is, of course, the Thais themselves.

History indicates that Thais were living in a land now known as Kiangsu-Shantung, in China, as far back as forty-five hundred years ago, but apparently they did not begin their southward drift until about a thousand years ago. Then, in 1256, they came south in great waves, as a result of the harassment of Kublai Khan and his armies, though some remained in China, where even today there are Thai-speaking peoples.

Once the great migrations of Thais had settled in the land that today is Thailand, they succeeded in overthrowing its Mon and Khmer (Cambodian) rulers and established the capital of the first Thai kingdom at Sukhothai. In the following century, a new capital was founded at Ayudhya, which lay four hundred miles to the south. Then, in 1767, when Ayudhya was destroyed by the Burmese, the capital of the nation (which was then called Siam) once again moved south, down the Chao Phya River to Bangkok, where it has remained.

As a result of their long history, the Thais have a rich and independent culture, though they have been strongly influenced by both China, whence they came, and India, which gave them their religion.

THAILAND ✻

Buddhism and Hinduism came from India at about the time of the Thai "Long March" south from China. At the present time, Thailand is perhaps the most devoutly Buddhist nation on earth.

It is a constitutional monarchy, with a king who has a taste for jazz and sailing, and a queen who is considered to be one of the most beautiful women in the world. In 1932, a bloodless revolution ended what had been an absolute monarchy, and today the political powers of His Majesty King Bhumiphol Adulyadej are in theory limited by the constitution, and the country is ruled by a central government—though much of the real power lies in the hands of what we have learned to call the military establishment. Despite inevitable unrest, however, I believe that most Thais, like most Japanese, retain a profound respect for their monarch, a respect that survives from earlier days when the monarch was given the reverence due a god.

Thailand is, in more ways than one, a fortunate country. It has always been a land of plenty. A stone inscription describing the first Thai kingdom reads, in part: "This Sukothai is good. In the water, there is fish; in the fields, there is rice. The King takes no advantage of the people. Whoever wants to trade, trades. The faces of the people shine bright with happiness." It is a description that is in large part still true today.

She exports rice, rubber, tin, maize, teak, tapioca, jute products, and—most famous of all—silk. Elephants, which were once one of her main export items, are no longer even listed in official trade figures. There are still plenty of elephants in the country, however, and they do important work in Thailand's lucrative teak forests.

Thailand has been lucky also in that she was the only nation in Southeast Asia to withstand the flood of European imperialism in the nineteenth century. Of course it was not only good luck that preserved Thailand's independence: they were aided, in their dealings with the great European powers, especially the French and the British, by their diplomatic skills. "As diplomats," writes the Asian historian, D. G. E. Hall, "the Thais have never been surpassed." King Mongut is a well-known example of this remarkable ability.

Perhaps no city in the world has grown so fast or changed so drastically in the two centuries of its life as the city of Bangkok. After the destruction of Ayudhya, in 1767, King Taksin set up his capital in Thonburi, on the other side of the river from Bangkok, which was then a small trading town. It was not until fifteen years later, when Rama I became king, that he decided to create his new capital at Bangkok—yet less than a hundred years later an English traveler wrote that Bangkok is a "floating city. . . of aquatic abodes and amphibious-looking inhabitants. . . where the dwellings of the people are for the most part afloat on rafts, and it is impossible at first sight to distinguish where land begins and where it ends." In less than a hundred years Bangkok had earned the appellation of "Venice of the East."

But no one could call her that now. Most of her canals have been filled in and transformed into roads, not many of the old houses are still standing, and much of the Bangkok that was built up in that first century has been destroyed in the second. In its place have come great new Western-style hotels with English-language names and American prices, air-conditioned movie houses, expensive night clubs, and restaurants of all nationalities. Residents of Bangkok and visitors to the city may eat an Italian pizza, an Indian curry, some Japanese sushi, or some Hungarian goulash; they may patronize German delicatessens, French cafés, American "Whimpy Bars," or an English pub; and there are, of course, innumerable Thai and Chinese restaurants catering to almost any size pocketbook.

The dollar is accepted currency almost everywhere, including many parts of the Floating Market, which has been commercialized to an exasperating degree and which, as a result, is an important source of foreign exchange for the country. According to the Tourist Organization of Thailand, more than three hundred and fifty thousand tourists and seventy thousand American servicemen visited the country during 1967, bringing in nearly a billion *baht* (almost fifty million dollars).

Yet despite all these modern "embellishments," Bangkok has by no means lost all its oriental charm. In the outlying districts one may still paddle down small, leaf-strewn canals (called *klongs*), stop at neighborhood floating markets, and admire pretty wooden houses perched on stilts over the water. Many children still take the river bus to school; bare-breasted women with betel-stained mouths still bathe unconcernedly in the river; yellow-robed monks still paddle themselves from house to house along the *klongs* making their daily collection of food.

The heart of the city that Rama I created back in the eighteenth century was, of course, his palace, which was surrounded by many resplendent *wats* (actually monasteries though they are usually referred to as temples) and which stood within the old city walls. Though the walls have been largely torn down now, to make way for more "profitable" structures, the Grand Palace and the *wats* remain as testaments to the heights that Siamese culture attained.

Within the square mile encompassed by the white, crenellated walls of the palace were the royal living quarters which the monarchs of Siam were to make their home for nearly two centuries, their reception halls and minor palaces as well as the court of justice and two famous and extremely beautiful *wats*: the Temple of the Emerald Buddha and the Temple of the Reclining Buddha. The reigning king now lives in Chitrlada Palace, in north Bangkok, but despite this fact and despite the fact also that certain additions have been made since the time of Rama I, the Grand Palace is essentially what it was two centuries ago when it was built by teams of conscript laborers to realize the dreams of the founder of the Chakri dynasty.

It is far beyond the scope of this book (and the ability of its author) to attempt a detailed account of the origins and development of the fantastic Siamese architectural style that evolved under the nine monarchs of the Chakri dynasty. But let us stand for a moment in the main courtyard of the Temple of the Emerald Buddha. It is, as always in Bangkok, hot, and the sun is now directly overhead. The paved courtyard is surrounded by strange, multicolored buildings, from whose gold-encrusted walls and roofs tiled in gleaming green and orange porcelain the rays of the sun overhead glimmer and dance—and one feels, for a moment, as though one had taken some hallucinogenic drug.

The roofs resemble giant, elaborately tiered wedding cakes, with layer upon layer of overlapping eaves. From each gable, golden carved wood curves upward to a point, rather like the horn of the mythical unicorn. Rising from the ground are stone spires, studded with chips of colored glass and china; a golden steeple glitters against the hot blue sky. Giant figures of demons peer down with terrifying faces, while strange ghoulish creatures that seem as though they must have come from a timeless Siamese fairy tale stare unblinking from shadowy corners. Somewhere the temple bells are tinkling gently in the breeze; from within the buildings comes the mingled odor of variously scented incense.

If it is the first time you have visited the Temple of the Emerald Buddha, the experience is not one you will soon forget. And the Buddha itself—the reason for this glorious extravagance of form and color? The image is twenty-two inches high and is carved—not of emerald of course—but of one solid piece of green jasper; its origins are as mysterious as its enigmatic smile. According to Prince Chula Chakrabongse, who wrote a history of the Chakri dynasty,* the stone itself probably came from the Caucasus and was sculptured in northern India by a Greek who stayed behind after Alexander the Great moved on. Then, during the next thousand years, the image must have moved from India to Ceylon and Burma and finally to what is now Thailand. Its first appearance in history is in 1436, in the northern town of Chiangrai, when the plaster in which it was encased was struck by lightning. In Southeast Asia, until quite recently, valuable Buddhas would be hidden in this way to conceal them from invading armies, which would otherwise carry them off as plunder. In 1778, General Chakri (who was later to be King Rama I) found the Emerald Buddha in Vientiane and brought it in triumph to the capital of Siam, where it has, ever since, been the country's most revered treasure.

Not far from the Temple of the Emerald Buddha stands the Grand Palace, which is best known to English readers because of

*Prince Chula Chakrabongse, *Lords of Life* (London: Alvin Redman, 1960).

Anna and the King of Siam and to the whole world because of *The King and I*—to the whole world, that is, except Thailand, where the film has been banned as an insult to the memory of the nation's most beloved monarch, King Mongut.

Anna Leonowens was an English governess who spent six years at the court of Siam educating some of the king's eighty-two children and some of his thirty-five wives. The memoirs she wrote on her return describe life at King Mongut's court in vivid, if not always accurate, detail. She was, after all, a Victorian, and could hardly have been expected to present a man who had thirty-five wives to the Victorian world without appropriate expressions of righteous indignation. Sometimes her indignation carries her away: of one of the palace harems, for instance, she writes:

Peering into the twilight, studiously contrived, of dimly-lighted and suggestive shadows, we discover in the centre of the hall a long line of girls with skins of olive—creatures who in years and physical proportions are yet but children, but by training developed into women and accomplished actresses. There are some twenty of them, in transparent draperies with golden girdles, their arms and bosoms, wholly nude, flashing, as they wave and heave, with barbaric ornaments of gold. The heads are modestly inclined, the hands are humbly folded, and the eyes droop timidly beneath long lashes. Their only garment, the lower skirt, floating in light folds about their limbs is of a very costly material bordered heavily with gold. On the ends of their fingers they wear long "nails" of gold, tapering sharply like the claws of a bird. . . . How I have pitied those ill-fated sisters of mine, imprisoned without a crime! If they could have rejoiced once more in the freedom of the fields and woods, what new births of gladness might have been theirs,— they who with a gasp of despair and moral death first entered those royal dungeons, never again to come forth alive!

THAILAND ✻

Margaret Langdon based her book, *Anna and the King of Siam*, on Anna Leonowens' highly colored memoirs; and *The King and I*, in its successive incarnations, was based on Margaret Langdon's book. Each creation was progressively further removed from reality, and the Thais bitterly resented the fact that the film, while claiming to be factual, presented one of the most enlightened monarchs of the nineteenth or indeed any other century as a doddering old man with a wholly unfactual penchant for his children's governess.

Not only was Mongut the first ruler in Southeast Asia's long history who could write and speak English, but he also found the time to study not only theology (for he was a monk before he ascended the throne) but also geography, history, mathematics, and astronomy. On one well-known occasion he astonished his court by predicting a total eclipse of the sun. Sir John Bowring, the British envoy who negotiated a treaty with him, wrote of his private apartments that "they were filled with various instruments, philosophical and mathematical, a great variety of Parisian clocks and pendules, thermometers, barometers, in a word, all the instruments and appliances which might be found in the study or library of any opulent philosopher in Europe."

During his reign, which lasted from 1851 to 1868, he was responsible for no less than five hundred laws and decrees, many of which he drafted himself. Among them were a proclamation that women were to marry only of their own free will, a provision to reduce the practice of conscripting labor, acts providing for the construction of canals and roads, and the setting up of a committee for the study of Thai history. "One cannot but wonder," wrote the historian, Prince Chula, somewhat wryly, "how he fitted in any time for his family life."

Hardly less remarkable as a reformer and lawmaker was Mongut's son and successor, King Chulalongkorn, who was responsible —among a number of important acts—for the peaceful abolition of slavery in Siam. At the same time, this fifth ruler of the Chakri dynasty was an even more uxorious man than his father: he had ninety-two wives, some of whom were his half-sisters.

✸ ✸

Opposite the Grand Palace is the Pramane Ground, which in older days was used as a saddling-up area for elephants. Now the only saddling on the Pramane Ground is done by children, who rent bicycles by the hour—for the ground is now a public park. It is used for various sports and ceremonies and is the scene of a large, animated weekend market.

Among the sports that are played there is one that is peculiarly Thai—that of "kite-fighting." On any evening during March and April—the kite-fighting season—the spectator may watch giant kites circling about in the sky and swooping down at one another, rather like combat planes engaged in a dogfight, though the only fatalities here are the paper kites and the rules are far older and perhaps even more complicated.

There are two contestants: the large and sturdy male kite, called a *chula*, and the smaller, more graceful female, the *pakpao*. Each kite is manipulated by a team of a dozen or so strong-armed men, who attempt to trap their opponents' kite in the sky and drag it down onto their territory. The *chula* is equipped with barbs, while the *pakpao* has a large loop, and customarily it is the *chula* that ventures into the *pakpao*'s airspace, the wily *pakpao* preferring to engage her man in her own territory. Spectators make bets on the outcome of the fight, which is often determined not so much by the skill of the fighters as by a sudden shift in wind of which one team will take immediate and decisive advantage.

Another traditional Thai sport that is played at the Pramane Ground around the same time of year is *takraw*, which makes use of a basket, placed higher than in basketball, into which a wicker ball is knocked with any part of the body except the hands. Again as in basketball, scoring is based on the number of times the ball is netted within a given period, with the difference that points are awarded according to the difficulty of the shot. The maximum number of points goes to the player who kicks the ball with his instep through a ring made by his arms, which he holds in front of his body, with the hands touching. Teams from companies and government offices compete in regular *takraw* tournaments.

In May, at the beginning of the rainy season and just before rice planting, the Pramane Ground is the scene of the Ploughing Ceremony, one of Thailand's most colorful pageants, which is always performed in the presence of the king. It apparently serves a double purpose—that of placating the gods, in the hope that they will grant a good crop of rice, and, at the same time, that of predicting whether they will or not. Like many other Thai customs, the Ploughing Ceremony has its origin in India, where similar rites take place.

In Thailand it begins at dawn, when Brahmins carry Buddhist and Hindu images in solemn procession to the Pramane Ground. There candles and incense are lit, and special delicacies—such as boiled and decorated pigs' heads—are offered to the gods. Then two sacred white oxen, draped in cloth of gold and with red-clad attendant grooms, enter the ground, dragging the ceremonial plough. The priests sprinkle lustral water, women in traditional costume scatter rice seeds from gold and silver pails, and the oxen plough the ground to the beat of antique brass drums and the eerie wailing of conch shells.

After the procession has circled the ploughing ground three times, the oxen are drawn up in front of the king, where they are offered their choice of seven different foods—various kinds of grain, beans, and liquor. Whether the harvest will be a good one depends on which food the oxen choose first. The worst possible choice they can make, auguring an abominable harvest, is the liquor.

Once the gods have made manifest their intentions, the ceremony is officially over, the national anthem is played, and the king is driven slowly away. It is at this moment that the visitor is well advised to keep his distance, for the barriers that had been holding back the throng of spectators are lowered, and the people stampede onto the ploughing ground. Everyone, it seems, has gone mad: men, women, and children are all groveling in the sacred ploughing ground, sifting the earth through their fingers.

But there is method in their madness, after all. They are looking for grains of rice that have just been sown. Mixed with ordinary rice at planting time, so the farmers believe, this "lucky" rice ensures a good harvest, and many farmers come from distant provinces in the hope of finding and carrying home a grain or two. Once the visitor has seen with his own eyes the violence of the stampede, he will have no doubt that the Thais do indeed take their Ploughing Ceremony seriously.

The same is true of almost all their ceremonies, of which they have a great many and for which they have a special flair and a special fondness. Throughout the Thai year, there are temple fairs, merit-making celebrations, festivals on Buddhist holidays, rites to propitiate the gods of rain, prayers to ask blessings on a newly built house, combined Hindu and Buddhist formalities to mark births, marriages (including the preparation of the bridal bed), and deaths, rites intended to frighten away evil spirits, ceremonial presentations of yellow robes to monks, and ordination ceremonies for Thai men when they become "temporary" monks.

Of all Thai pageants, perhaps the most splendid is the Royal Tod Kathin, when the king's long, stately barges, rowed by handsomely garbed oarsmen, glide downriver to the Temple of Dawn. Then, in November, there is Loi Krathong night, during which thousands of tiny paper boats carrying flowers and candles are floated down the river: the bobbing lights reflected in the water have all the fleeting charm and wonder of Japanese cherry blossom viewing. The April Songkran water-throwing festival is a gay, boistrous celebration—and certainly the world's wettest.

Water, as the reader will have noted, plays a tremendous role in Thai life, even now when so many of the *klongs* have been filled in and turned into roads. One reason, of course, is that rice, the staple of the country, requires great quantities of water; the fertility of the country is directly dependent on plentiful rainfall. Another consideration is that until quite recently most traveling was done by way of water rather than land.

Thailand's chief waterway, which winds through the central alluvial plain like a long, sinuous snake and on the east bank of which Bangkok lies, is the Menam Chao Phya, often known simply as the Menam, for *menam* or *mae nam* means "river" in Thai. It flows down from the northern hills to the central plain, emptying into the Gulf of Siam, and is as vital to Thailand as the Nile is to Egypt. On the west bank lies Thonburi, which for sixteen years, between the Bangkok and Ayudhya eras, was the capital of the country. Now the two cities are linked by three important bridges and are usually referred to collectively as Bangkok. Visitors to the city always remember Thonburi for its Floating Market, its stately Temple of Dawn, and its picturesque little canals.

Bangkok's Chinatown, where I first stayed on my arrival, has no wide avenues or gorgeous temples: it is a maze of narrow streets and terraced houses of but two stories. Unlike Hong Kong, which rises out of its rocky floor in vast, multistoried buildings, Chinatown—like the rest of Bangkok—is built on mud, which makes the erection of tall structures both difficult and extremely expensive.

Chinatown, therefore, tends to avoid them: it is squat and squalid, a nineteenth-century swamp of life and teeming variety; a jungle of rice and tea shops, tailors and jewelers, barbers and apothecaries who sell the immemorial remedies of the Celestial Kingdom—dried frogs, bottled snakes, powdered horn, and the like; panoramic collages of giant signboards; streetside family workshops making steel brackets or fittings or spare parts for sewing machines; massage parlors and striptease theaters and Chinese opera companies from Hong Kong; restaurants that serve excellent Chinese food and beggars waiting patiently beside the doorway; boys selling pictures of bosomy beauties and naked children playing an oriental version of hopscotch; Chinese temples with heavy stucco roofs—a nightmare of smells and heat and dust and traffic jams.

THAILAND ✻

The Chinese and the Thais have been intimately related ever
since the first Thai tribes migrated south from China and established
their own kingdom. From then until the Communists took power in
Peking, there was constant trade between mainland Chinese and
their cousins to the south. This economic coöperation, during all
those centuries, combined with intermarriage to produce a generally
harmonious relationship between the two peoples.

At the present time, about half of the residents of Bangkok
are Chinese—in the sense that they speak Chinese dialects and
observe Chinese customs, although most of them have Thai nation-
ality and speak Thai as well as Chinese. The percentage of people
with some Chinese ancestry is much higher, probably around eighty
percent—and this includes the royal house. Today the government imposes restrictions on the number of Chinese who can come
to live in the country, as it does on all nationalities, but people usually find that there are ways around the restrictions.

The differences suggest the—perhaps unconscious—division
of labor that has grown up between the two peoples. The Thais,
having no particular taste for commerce, tend to leave it increasingly
in Chinese hands; at the same time, the Chinese leave the politics
and administration of their country to the Thais. Of overseas
Chinese, the statement has often been made: "They don't mind who
holds the head of the cow providing they can milk it." But if this is
true of the Chinese, it seems to be equally true of other foreign residents of Bangkok. There are large, and prosperous, communities of
Indians, Americans, British, Japanese, and, indeed, of most nationalities. There are few restrictions on capital investment, labor is cheap,
labor laws are lax, and business is booming. In Bangkok today large
profits find their way into foreign as well as domestic pockets.

2. *Wat Benjamabopit,* called
the Marble Temple, was built
at the turn of the century
out of Italian marble in the
classic Thai style; Bangkok
has three hundred *wats.*

3. *Kinnari,* part woman, part bird, is one of numerous mythological creatures at the Temple of the Emerald Buddha in Bangkok.

4. *Ploughing Ceremony* is one of the
most colorful of Thailand's many
annual pageants: here, oxen are being
brought into the presence of the king,
who always attends the ceremony.

5. *Classical dances* vary from one part of the country to another; the girl dancers enact famous myths and legends.

6. *Flower market* in Bangkok, show-
ing a girl weaving a wreath of jasmine
blossoms that may be used as personal
decoration (like the girl on the front
cover), or may be offered as homage
to the Buddha.

7. *Children* in Thailand, even the poorest, usually have a happy childhood and never quite lose their sense of fun—which helps account for the country's reputation as the "Land of Smiles."

8. *Beautiful beaches* abound on Thailand's convoluted coastline; many are almost completely unspoiled, for foreign tourists haven't found them yet, and native Thais are only just beginning to appreciate sunbathing and swimming in the sea.

9. *Though much modernized*, Bangkok boasts many a private garden luxuriant with palm trees and tropical plants.

10. *Rajadamnern Avenue,* with the Golden Mount Temple and the remains of the old city walls in the background.

11. *Traffic policeman* is dwarfed by giant signboards advertising a popular, locally made, low-budget movie. Bangkok's cars are mostly Japanese.

12. *National Assembly Hall*, built to house the throne room, is now the seat of the National Parliament; in the foreground is a *samlor*, the common three-wheeled taxi.

13. *Democracy Monument* (on Rajadamnern Avenue) commemorates the 1932 bloodless revolution that ended absolute monarchy.

14. *Bus stop* near Grand Palace: the absence of subways means buses are almost always overcrowded.

15. *Grand Palace,* shown here in the the early morning, was built by the founder of the Chakri dynasty some two centuries ago. Pramane Ground, in front of the palace, is a recreation area for the citizens of Bangkok as well as the scene of a busy weekend market.

16. *Chakri Hall,* in the Grand Palace, once part of royal living quarters, is now used mainly for state receptions and banquets.

17—18. *Interior views* of the Grand Palace, where Thai monarchs once lived with their many wives and children and where Anna met the King of Siam.

19—20. *Temple of the Emerald Buddha,* within the palace compound, has pavilions roofed with gleaming porcelain tiles and decorated with brilliant gilt carvings; the grotesque giant figures are said to keep evil spirits away.

21. *Monkey warrior,* from Emerald Buddha Temple, is a figure in the Hindu Ramayana epic.

22. *Legendary lion,* from the same temple, is typical *wat* sculpture.

23. *Figurehead* of one of the royal barges is also a monkey warrior.

24—25. *Wat Arun* ("The Temple of Dawn") was built in 18th century and is decorated with bits of Chinese porcelain.

26. *Ploughing maidens* carry sacred rice to persuade the gods to grant a good harvest.

27. *Procession* of Brahmins (Hindu priests) crosses Pramane Ground in the annual ceremony.

28. *Spectators* stampede, at end of ceremony, to find grains of "lucky" rice.

29. *Drums,* conch shells, and other native instruments provide music for the ceremony.

32. *Open market* at Pramane Ground.

33. *Sweets for sale!*—a common Bangkok scene.

34. *Curries* are varied, spicy, and very hot.

35. *Essentials* are both red and green peppers.

36. *Some flowers* bring good fortune; others, bad. Let the buyer beware!

53

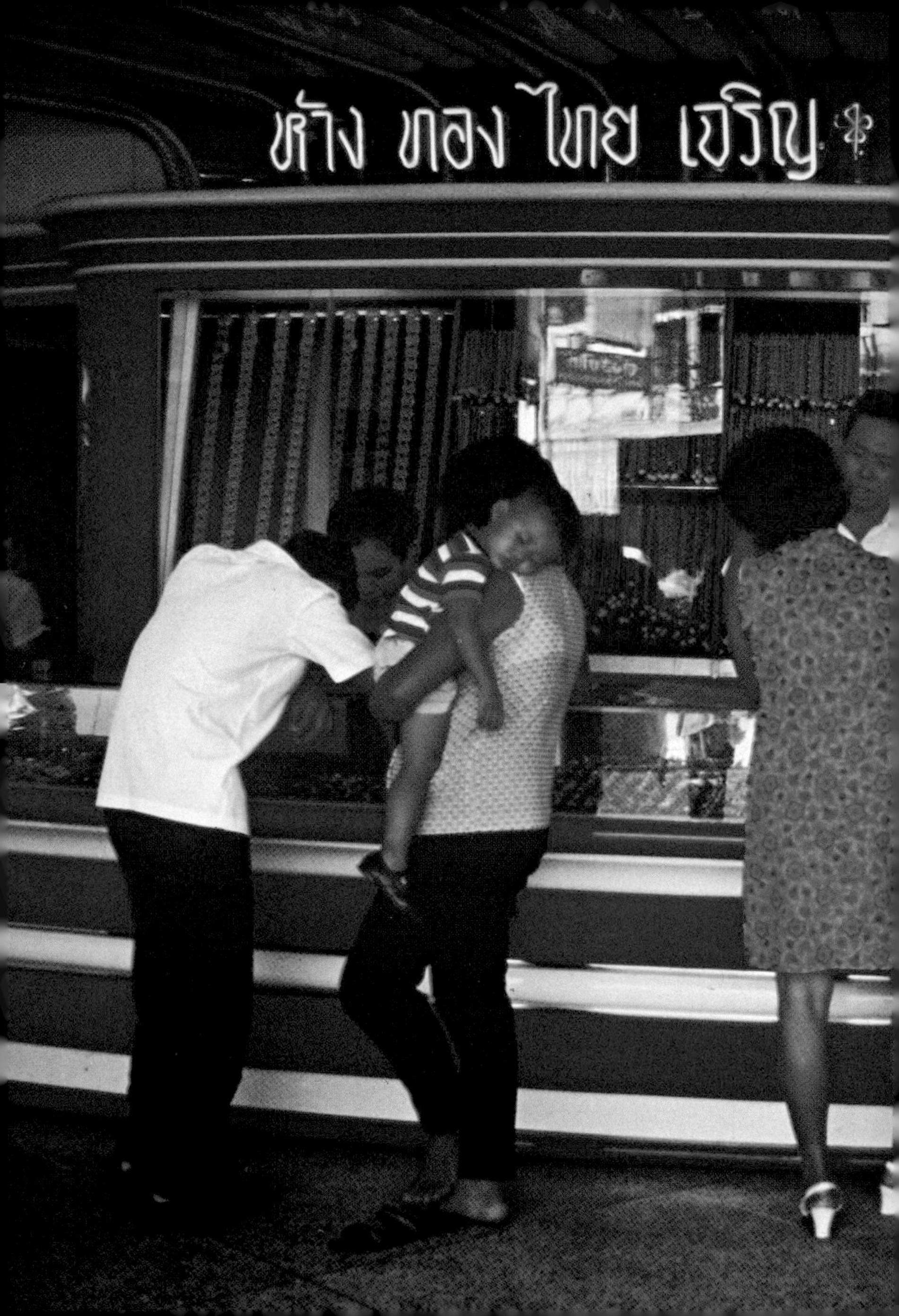
ห้าง ทอง ไทย เจริญ

37. *Gold merchant's shop* in Chinatown is crowded, for Thais—out
of long tradition—would rather
put their money in gold than in
banks.

38. *Traffic jams* are a permanent
condition of life in Bangkok's
Chinatown.

39. *Cigarettes* and lottery
tickets are both govern-
ment monopolies in Thai-
land.

42. *Tar Tien market,* on the ▶
Bangkok side of the river, starts
early in the morning; in the
background is the Temple of
Dawn.

40. *The samlor driver's* job
is doomed: because of traffic congestion, these three-
wheeled vehicles must
eventually be replaced in
Bangkok by ordinary taxis.

41. *Monk* carries his alms
bowl at dawn through Bangkok's half-deserted streets;
throughout the country,
Buddhist Thais provide food
for monks daily.

57

Out into the country

"But if you really want to know Thailand," a man at the *Bangkok Post* told me, "get out of the city and do some traveling up-country. After all, eighty percent of the workers in Thailand are engaged in agriculture, and a third of the national income is derived from agriculture. As far as exports go, eighty-five percent are agricultural products. And what's more, most of Thailand's urgent problems are rooted in the countryside. That's where you'll get to know the real people of the country, and the real problems they've got to face." Accordingly, I made arrangments to take a short holiday from the newspaper—the month was July—and to go up the River Kwai to the Three Pagoda Pass, on the Burmese border. Accompanying me would be Damrong Suksri, an engineering student from Chulalongkorn University, who wanted us to make our first stop at his aunt's house, outside Thonburi, where ceremonies were to be held to celebrate his cousin's ordination as a monk. We agreed to meet early in the morning at the landing stage near the Tar Tien market, where we could get the boat to Thonburi.

Bangkok is at its best at dawn, and for a number of reasons, not the least of them being that this is the time the shaven-headed monks file from their temples with their food bowls to gather alms.

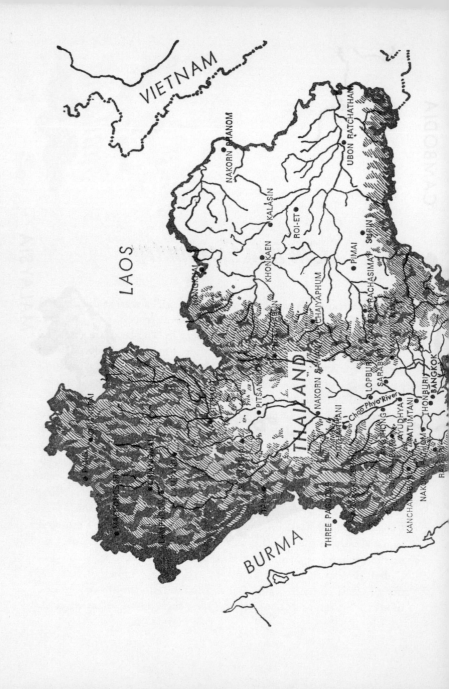

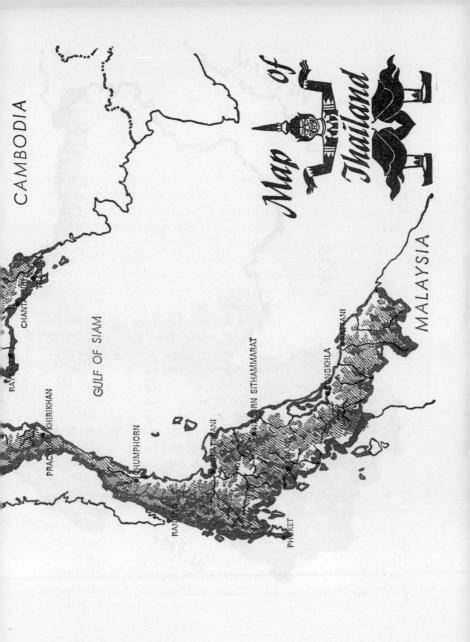

THAILAND ✵

I found it an affecting sight to watch the barefoot monk, his head bowed low, move silently through the half-deserted streets, stopping every now and then at an open doorway or at the entrance of a shop to receive food. The monk himself says nothing; his face remains grave and his eyes lowered as he continues silently on while the alms-giver expresses his gratitude by pressing his palms together in front of his forehead in the traditional Thai gesture. Almsgiving is a way of "making merit"—and merit making, according to the Buddhist doctrine of Karma, is the way to ensure that things go well in the next incarnation.

By six-thirty, when I arrived at Tar Tien, the river itself was already bustling with boats and barges of all sizes and shapes, and commuters from the residential areas of Thonburi were scurrying away from the ferryboats toward their offices in exactly the same way that people in other cities flock out of subways and commuter trains in the morning rush hours. Thais are early risers! At the market, food was already being unloaded from barges and boats, and in another hour the stalls would be heaped with bright-colored fruits and vegetables, fresh from the country, and with fish and meat; vendors would be hawking their wares; trucks would be shunting noisily into position to load up for city deliveries.

As our long-nosed river-taxi surged across the yellow, choppy waters of the Chao Phya, we had to open the paper umbrellas that had been given us as protection against the spray. We skimmed past the grey hulls of two cruisers of the Royal Thai Navy, past Thammersart University, past sawmills, warehouses, and factories, past Siriraj Hospital, then across the path of a long line of barges pulled by a single tugboat. . . and found ourselves in the calm waters of the Bangkok Noi canal. We shut our umbrellas and put them away, and as our taxi skimmed through Thonburi, the scene reminded me of my first glimpse of Thailand. Weathered, wooden houses perched on stilts on either side of the *klong* (brown, laughing children splashing and swimming and jumping from trees into the water; a bargee poling his sluggish craft under a bridge.

As we left Thonburi and sailed deeper into the country, I become more sharply aware that we were, after all, in a tropical land. Coconuts, pomelos, mangoes, bananas, oranges, pomegranates, and papayas grew luxuriously along the banks, where there were now fewer houses, and in the branches of the trees, mynas, kingfishers, bluejays, koels, warblers, owls, and parrots piped and whistled, squeaked and squawked. In a garden, a pet gibbon swung from the branch to which he was chained; buffaloes grazed in the flat fields; large fishing nets hung over the water. "In the water," I thought, "there is fish; in the fields, there is rice. . . ."

The rest of the quotation came true too: the faces of the people shone bright with happiness. Damrong's aunt—my hostess—was a round, jolly woman who laughed a great deal, and, as she did, one could see that chewing betel nut had stained her mouth bright red. She looked like one of the women I had seen sitting under umbrellas in the Bangkok markets—and that, as it turned out, is exactly what she was: a market woman. Later Damrong took me to see the large orchard behind the house, rich in pineapple, mango, and durian. I had no doubt that the proceeds of the market garden were extremely useful in meeting the family budget, for Damrong's uncle was a civil servant, a notoriously underpaid class in Thailand.

The house itself was typical of those we had seen on our way up the canal: a one-story building made of wood, with an iron roof, standing on piles over the *klong*. A short flight of steps led

THAILAND ✱

from the water to a long open veranda. Inside, the house was dark
and so a little cooler. Cushions were grouped on the floor around
a low table in the main living area; in the family shrine sticks of incense and flowers were arranged before a small image of the Buddha;
large, faded photographs of the king and queen in gilt frames hung
on the plain wood wall; and there was a television set. The sleeping

area, with mattresses and mosquito nets strung from the ceiling, stood a few steps above the living area but was not divided from it. At the back of the house were the kitchen and toilet.

By this time around a dozen people, mostly relatives and friends, had already arrived, and we sat on the veranda, eating and talking as the afternoon turned to evening. Despite the fact that there were far too many mosquitoes for comfort, it is one of my pleasantest memories of Thailand—and I noticed, incidentally, that the Thais seemed to be bothered far less than I by the beasts. We drank *oleeung* that was delivered by the coffee boat, and we ate *kwaiteeo* that was brought by the noodle boat, and we sampled fruit from the orchard behind the house.

It was on that afternoon that I first tasted durian. I had, of course, often seen the fruit in the market but, like most foreigners, had been put off trying it because (to use the words of the Oxford Dictionary) of its "strong civet odour." However, the fruit was homegrown here, it was part of the scene, and I felt a moral obligation to try it. I understood then why the deliciously rich, creamy fruit is so highly prized (and priced) in Thailand. To a Thai, the durian is as great a delicacy as the truffle is to a Frenchman; the best varieties may cost as much as three or four dollars, and even poor Thais will often spend disproportionately large parts of their income on the fruit.

Then, even if you have made your mind up to buy and eat one, you will not—unless you have long years of experience behind you —be able to tell whether an unopened durian is in the right stage to be eaten. Further, you need expertise to open it properly: you must split the hard outer shell with a hatchet, then pry the fruit open with your hands, taking care neither to damage the pulp inside nor impale your fingers on the spikes outside. Yet I decided in favor of it, despite all its disadvantages; it has, by the way, one further one: it is found nowhere else in the world but Southeast Asia.

I was asked, as one often is in Thailand, if I wanted to take a bath in the river; and the Thai climate being what it is, I happily accepted the invitation, as one usually does. The technique of bathing publicly in a river is not quite the same as having a shower in the privacy of your own bathroom. The Thais have solved the problem by making use of two long lengths of cotton cloth (called *pakuma*). You wrap one *pakuma* around you and strip beneath it, then fasten it around your waist and go into the river for your bath. After you come out, you wrap the second, dry *pakuma* around you and slip the wet one off underneath. Once you are dry (which does not take very long in the Thai climate), you dress again and are ready for the evening's festivities—which were to include, on this occasion, the ceremonial shaving of the hair and eyebrows of the prospective monk.

It is the laudable custom in Thailand for every man to become a monk for at least a few months of his life—usually for a period of three months between the ages of twenty-one and twenty-five. During those months, the temporary members of the monastery follow the same rules as the regular monks: they wear their yellow robes at all times; each morning they carry their alms bowls around the neighborhood to collect food; they must fast until midday, abstain from alcohol, and observe the law of chastity. A prospective monk is called *naga*, in token of the serpent which, in Buddhist legend, took human form and sought ordination.

Temporary monks are expected to use that three-month period of their lives to study and meditate on Buddhist doctrine—if the two words are not a contradiction in terms, for the Buddha himself asked people to accept nothing in blind faith, not even his own teaching. Nonetheless, there is a basic philosophy that pervades Buddhism, and it is this that the three-month period is intended to help make clear to the young man embarking on life: that suffering stems from desire; that only love and compassion can produce happiness. Thus, the more strongly influenced a people are by the Buddhist ideals, the more likely they are to be detached, unassertive, and gentle. That they may also, of course, be assiduous, hard-working, even determined, goes without saying.

Damrong's cousin faced the ordeal of having his head and eyebrows closely shaven with the utmost seriousness, but when the process was over and someone handed him a mirror, he could not repress a glance of astonishment, perhaps even of horror, at his new look—for there is nothing quite so naked as a close-shaven pate. However, he quickly pulled himself together as the ceremony continued. After a white robe was thrown over his shoulders, he lay prostrate on the floor in an attitude of prayer while relatives and friends made speeches suitable to the occasion. The *naga* was told how great were the efforts made on his behalf by his parents in order to rear him properly; he was lectured on the duties of a monk; he was spoken to of the teachings of the Buddha. And during these solemn speeches, the others in the room continued to smoke and drink, chattering all the while: it seemed to me an oddly informal background to so serious an occasion.

Informality was the keynote, also, of the ceremonies the following morning at the monastery. Around nine o'clock the procession started off for the *wat*: the *naga*, still in his white robe, was carried shoulder-high by his friends, under a large ceremonial umbrella to protect his newly shaven head from the sun; behind him came women bearing gifts for the monks—cigarettes, flowers, and chocolates, all wrapped in bright yellow cellophane; the procession was accompanied by a group of excited musicians beating Thai drums (called *klong-yao*) with happy fervor.

Before entering the monastery, they circled its main building (*bot*) three times: first, to honor the Lord Buddha himself; second, to honor his law (Dharma); and third, to honor the brotherhood of monks (Sangha). At the entrance to the *bot*, the *naga* threw coins to the crowd (mostly neighborhood children) to symbolize his rejection of the material world. Inside, some twenty orange-robed monks sat on the floor, awaiting him. Once he had entered, the ceremony itself was short. After a brief interrogation about the meaning of Buddhism, there was chanting by the monks; then they were given presents, and yellow robes were presented to the *naga*. In this way, Damrong's cousin embarked on his three-month quest for knowledge of the Buddha and his own nature which, it was hoped, would result in self-improvement.

✳　　✳

From Thonburi, the next day, we took a bus to Kanchanaburi, some seventy miles away. It is a dull, flat provincial town, similar to so many Thai villages—an untidy mixture of dusty roads and dirty canals, of peasant poverty and small-town prosperity. Woods and concrete buildings stand side-by-side; giant movie signboards elbow garish *wats*; noodle stalls are wedged between air-conditioned restaurants; there are open food markets and small, dark Chinese grocery shops. There are also pedicabs (which the Japanese call *rintaku*)—though these have been banned in the capital.

And there are a few concrete hotels, with air-conditioned rooms, but we chose to spend the night in a small wooden hotel where our room cost only a dollar. Considering the price, we were not surprised that the hotel was hot and dirty, that sanitation was crude and sound boomed and reverberated through the thin partitions that served as walls. I was kept awake a good part of the night by some hunters who had just returned from the jungle into which we were to go the following day and who kept talking and laughing about their adventures.

Kanchanaburi's chief claim to fame is the fact that it is the scene of the notorious bridge that was the subject of *The Bridge on the River Kwai*. And the bridge may still be seen today—though it is not the one that moviegoers saw, for the film was actually shot in Ceylon. There is a cemetery in Kanchanaburi for those who died in the making of the bridge and the railway; it is a moving experience to read the inscriptions on the gravestones.

During the war, the single-track "death railway" went all the way to Rangoon, but today it stops at the village of Nam Tok. From here on, the track has been carted away by neighborhood people, and the jungle has grown over the cleared space where the track lay, leaving no trace of the world's most infamous railway, which had cost so many lives.

There are no roads through the jungle after Nam Tok; the only way to continue our journey was by boat; but this being the rainy season, we were not sure how long we might have to wait for a boat going upriver. We were lucky however: we found a boat taking some men up to work in the forests about half-way to Sang-klaburi, a small settlement only a few miles from the Three Pagodas. We paid our share and joined the party.

THAILAND ✳

It was a long boat, very similar to the one we had taken when we left Bangkok, though the task of the driver was considerably more difficult here, for the swift-flowing Kwai River was swollen with rain from the mountains. It was raining when we embarked, and it continued to rain, which I regretted not only because we got soaked but also because it made photography so difficult—and the scenery was extremely beautiful, with tall, densely packed forests growing up from the banks of the river and rich green mountains in the background. Twice I saw elephants working in the forest, and several times, as we struggled upstream, we passed rafts floating down to Kanchanaburi. On the rafts, which were made of large logs lashed together, were small huts where the raftsman, and sometimes his family as well, lived.

The forest workers disembarked at a small village, and though we wanted to continue on to Sangklaburi, our boatman refused— on the grounds that, as it was still raining extremely hard, the river would be too dangerous. Perhaps if we had pressed more money on him, he might have changed his mind, but, as it was almost evening, we decided to spend the night where we were. Borrowing a couple of mosquito nets, we slept under a shelter on a wooden pontoon. It was not the most comfortable night I have ever spent.

Early the next morning we were lucky enough to catch a ride in a boat that was taking two villagers up to Sangklaburi. The weather was still bad: the green mountains into which we were heading were capped with clouds, and the river became ever more twisted and narrow as we continued up, and the current flowed faster against us. Approaching Sangklaburi, the boatman asked if we were going to the mission. We had no idea what sort of mission it might be, never having heard of it before, but as it was

still raining hard and as we had no other place to stay, we agreed
that the mission was where we were going.

"I wish you'd have come yesterday—we could have used your
blood." Despite the ominous sound of the words, however, with
which we were welcomed, I did not for a moment suppose that we
had stumbled onto a den of cannibals the day after a tribal feast—
for the words were spoken in a strong American accent by a smiling,
middle-aged woman dressed in the gray uniform of a volunteer
nurse. She continued: "We had a man die of malaria. If we'd had
the blood to give him a transfusion, we might have saved him."

One of the excitements of travel, of course, is meeting up with
the unexpected. Certainly neither Damrong nor I had had the
least idea, when we determined to make our journey to the Three
Pagodas, that we would come upon a Baptist Mission and a small
hospital in the upper reaches of the River Kwai; nor that we would
find ourselves singing a hymn before sitting down to a dinner of
as near Western food as our hostess could make it; nor that after-
wards we would sleep between real sheets. Our hostess was Mrs.
Paul Dodge, and her husband was the missionary in charge.

During the course of dinner, we heard a good deal from the Rev.
Paul Dodge about the area, which he described as a desolate and
disease-ridden no-man's-land, a place where no one wanted to come
save fugitives from justice—who had no choice, smugglers and
Burmese rebels, hunters of course—and missionaries. The smugglers take radios, watches, and other luxury goods from Thailand
into Burma; and sometimes they are able to capture government

elephants in Burma, which they smuggle into Thailand, where they fetch a good price.

The Burmese rebels often engage in smuggling in order to make money to buy arms, and they are active in organizing resistance, particularly among the Karen tribesmen, to the present Burmese regime. These rebels contribute substantially to the nagging problem of insurgency and resistance with which the Rangoon government is constantly faced. Fugitives and escaped convicts, the Rev. Dodge told us, may be found working the teak forests.

On the subject of the hunters, he was more cheerful—for he himself is one. There was plenty of wild game in the district, he said, including a number of very rare jungle cats. The many skins on the teakwood floor of the Dodges' large log cabin, built on their arrival about seven years before, gave ample evidence that the missionary was no mean shot. He told us it was his ambition to bag a tiger before he left.

Despite the inadequacy of the hospital facilities, the Dodges have been far more successful saving lives than souls. "The only people we seem to convert," the missionary said frankly, "are the ones who think they can get a job in the mission hospital if they become Christians." The plain fact is, of course, that Buddhists are generally content to remain Buddhists and see no reason for change. The Rev. Dodge agreed. And without directly criticizing Buddhism, he implied that he found it a "complacent" religion. Considering the urgent health problems of the area, one had no difficulty understanding what he meant. I was reminded of what King Mongut is said to have told his missionary friends: "What you teach them to *do* is admirable, but what you teach them to *believe* is foolish."

Indeed, there is a sad lack of medical care available to the people of the district. The small mission hospital is the only one within many miles, and it is run almost single-handedly by Mrs. Dodge. Malaria is an extremely common complaint among the widely scattered inhabitants of the jungle, as is plain malnutrition, and at times the mission hospital was so crowded, Mrs. Dodge said, patients had to sleep in the corridors. There were serious shortages in almost every department, from drugs to doctors; the blood supply, as Mrs. Dodge announced when we arrived, was completely dry. More than any other hospital I have ever seen, this little Baptist Mission hospital seemed like an emergency medical unit on a badly mauled battlefront.

The following morning we started off on foot along jungle paths toward the Burmese border. Luckily we were accompanied by a young Burmese; otherwise I doubt whether we would ever have found our way. He had recently left Rangoon, he said, and was on his way to Bangkok, where he hoped somehow to get to America. I feared that his chances, without either passport or money, were very slim indeed.

The narrow path through the jungle was wet and slippery and sometimes seemed simply to disappear. For a short stretch, the path paralleled the old, vanished railway, and at one point we stumbled over an old buffer, completely overgrown with creeper, on which we sat for a while and took photographs of ourselves. The young Burmese had brought a rifle along with him, but we saw nothing for him to shoot at, not even a snake.

After a fairly hard walk, we reached the Three Pagodas—our journey's end. They were crumbling white plaster edifices which seemed sadly out of place in the lush jungle. There was nobody

THAILAND ✳

around, and nothing else to mark the fact that this was the border between two countries. I wondered, idly, how far I would have got had I ventured on into Burma, or what might have happened to me, and I realized, as we stood in Thailand looking into Burma, that I had no intention of trying to find out.

We had attained our objective—the point where the trunk meets the head on the elephant-shaped map of Thailand. Three Pagodas in the deep jungle. There was nothing to do now but go back.

44. *Boatman* poles his barge under a bridge at Thonburi, Bangkok's sister city, on the opposite bank of the Chao Phya River, the great river of Thailand's central plain. Most rice (over eighty percent) is transported by river or canal.

45. *Topless bathing* in the river is older than history.

46. *Coffee vendor* sounds horn to announce his arrival.

47. *Waterside houses,* boats, and barges shelter over a third of the thirty-two million population.

48. *Coconut and rice cakes* provide a meal of sorts for this elderly woman.

49. *Durian* is the most expensive of Thai fruits; the yellow pulp inside the prickly rind has a disagreeably strong smell that belies its delicious flavor.

50. *River bus* takes students to school; competition is fierce to enter one of Thailand's seven universities.

51. *The seesaw* is universal—but the Thai smile is unique.

52. *Village school* is a crucial step toward prosperity; feudal till recently, Thailand now has a fast-growing middle class.

53. *Greengrocers* paddle their way from house to house; the character of the Thai cuisine demands a large variety of ingredients.

54. *Thailand* has nearly two thousand miles of inland waterways, and not all her boats are hand-powered; motor launch, below, provides swift transportation.

55. *Typical* Thai waterscape with wooden houses on stilts and pointed roofs, lush tropical vegetation, and the sluggish *klong* itself.

85

56—58. *Buffaloes* (*overleaf*) dislike cracked, dry earth—but the clouds on the horizon suggest rainy season is about to begin; below, a buffalo-drawn plough illustrates the traditional Thai method of rice cultivation; Thailand's seven million buffaloes are usually tended by children (opposite), who play with them and give them pet names.

59. *Paddy fields* are essential to Thailand's economy: rice is the staple food of the country as well as its chief export.

60. *Country buses* are sometimes still made of wood and invariably driven too fast; accidents are unhappily frequent.

61. *Cockfighting,* though banned in Bangkok, is a popular diversion in the countryside; betting changes during the course of the fight as the contestants demonstrate their valor and skill.

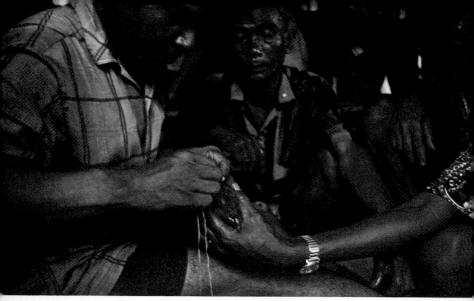

62. *Owner* of the fighting cock sews up its head-wounds between rounds so it will be able to see its opponent.

63. *Fishfighting* is also a popular country sport—and a more foolhardy one for the stranger to bet on.

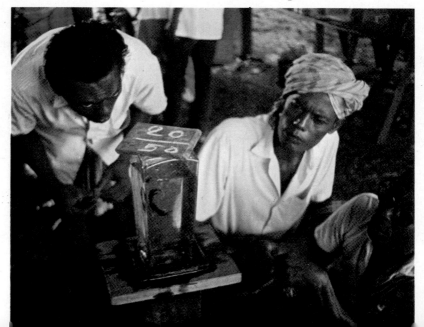

64. *Country fare:* chicken on bamboo skewers accompanied by soft drinks sold in plastic bags.

65. *Frogs,* fried with garlic, are considered a great delicacy.

66. *Beggars,* though common, are less frequently seen in Thailand than most of Southeast Asia.

67. *Thai men* who profess Buddhism become monks for a short period; before their ordination they are carried in procession around the monastery's courtyard.

68. *Musicians* play traditional Thai drums.

69. *Friends and relatives* bring gifts for the monks.

70. *Abbot* presents yellow robes to the new monks.

71. *River Kwai* flows down from Burma through a sparsely inhabited jungle area.

◄72—73. *Elephants* are invaluable not only in felling timber but also in shifting it to the river for transport.

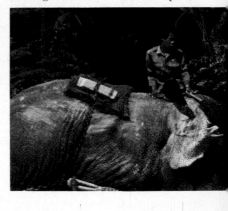

74. *Mon children,* near Burmese border, carry metal drums on their heads; Mons are one of Thailand's many minor ethnic groups.

75. *Mountain peaks* that separate
Thailand from Burma, in the upper
reaches of the River Kwai, are veiled
by clouds heralding a rainstorm.

Chiangmai and the North

I must note at once that travel in Thailand does not usually involve hardship of the sort I experienced on my trip to the Burmese border. Most of the larger towns have airports, and roads and railways extend over most of the country. The growing problem of insurgency, particularly in the northeast, has stimulated the Thai government as well as foreign aid agencies to invest in intensive road-building programs, if only to give added mobility to the army.

Even traveling by road, however, has its peculiar hazards, largely because motor transport is relatively new to the average Thai, who is inclined to handle buses and taxis as if they were bullock carts. Thais, for this reason, are sometimes referred to as "first-generation drivers." The country bus, the cheapest and most popular form of transport, is usually a dilapidated, wooden vehicle which is customarily driven at frightening speeds by a driver whose sole object appears to be either to intimidate or to impress his passengers. When the crash occurs (accidents on Thai roads are alarmingly and disproportionately frequent), the driver, if he is still mobile, invariably flees the scene before the police arrive.

But bus travel in Thailand also has its peculiar charm: when the journeys are long, passengers are likely to alleviate their boredom by sociable orgies of eating and drinking. Stops are frequent, and at every stop the bus is besieged by energetic vendors of foods of all sorts (I remember particularly a wonderfully spicy dried chicken on bamboo skewers) and varieties of soft drinks in plastic bags.

Train travel, incidentally, can be just as congenial—if not more so, since, for many Thais, a train journey is a wonderful excuse to get drunk. On overnight expresses, restaurant cars are crowded with people drinking either Singha beer or Mekhong, the cheap and very fiery local whiskey; the atmosphere is as friendly and rowdy as an English pub on Saturday night—or an American bar (so I am told) almost any time. An American AID officer, whom I met on a train from Bangkok to Chiangmai, told me he always traveled by train because of what he called the "restaurant entertainment" —though his first-class, single-berth, air-conditioned compartment cost him considerably more than an air ticket would have done.

I have noticed that conversation between Thais and foreigners on these sociable trains follows a familiar pattern. If you should happen to sit down at a table where there are already a few partly and agreeably intoxicated Thais, the first question is whether you speak the language. The question is in Thai, and you of course reply in Thai. "A little", you say. At this, there are smiles and laughter, and you are told that you speak Thai very well. Next you are asked what you think of Thai women (the people you are drinking with are, of course, all men). You reply that they are the most beautiful women in the world, which produces more laughter and shouts of "Good, good!" To every question about other aspects of life in Thailand—food, whiskey, countryside, temples—you reply, of course, that everything is wonderful. You add that you would like to marry a Thai girl and live in Thailand the rest of your life—

statements which, by that time, seem reasonably true. Then, flushed with your linguistic success, you call a waiter and order another bottle of Mekhong. At this evidence of good will, your companions are convinced that you speak Thai perfectly—though the chances are you now come to the end of your limited vocabulery. But— *mai penrai*! You have already assured yourself of an evening of enormous *snuk*.

✳   ✳

The train on which I met the American officer leaves Bangkok at five in the afternoon and arrives at Chiangmai at ten o'clock the following morning. During the night, it climbs from sea level to a thousand feet above, and it is not only the landscape that changes, from rivers and flat rice-fields to wooded hills. You step out of the train to a temperature which is far cooler than that of Bangkok, and you sense immediately a drop in humidity. Chiangmai, though it is Thailand's second largest city, boasts a population of only a hundred thousand.

Formerly a Lao state, Chiangmai is the name of a province as well as a city. The town itself was built in 1296 by command of King Mengrai because he had seen on the site two white samburs (a kind of elk), two barking deer, and a family of white mice. This combination was taken to be an omen indicative of great good fortune, though the subsequent turbulent history of the city would seem to belie the royal interpretation of the omen. Legend says further that the king conscripted ninety thousand men who worked round-the-clock shifts, completing the city of Chiangmai within a four-month period. Whether the latter legend be true or not, the workmen did not scamp their work, for most of the old walls are still in existence, as well as the defensive moat that surrounded them.

But walls and moat were powerless to repel Chiangmai's many conquerors. Strategically placed on the northern route for invading armies between Burma and Siam, the city was fought over for centuries by kings of the two countries. It changed hands frequently, now subject to Burma, now to Siam; and occasionally it attained the status of an independent city-state. The last battle for Chiangmai was fought in 1775, when King Taksin drove the Burmese out and the city became part of Siam—and has remained so ever since.

In many ways, it seemed to me, Chiangmai could well be compared to Kyoto, the ancient capital of Japan (though the population of Kyoto is ten times that of Chiangmai). But both cities, once strategically important, are now quiet and provincial, interesting to tourists because of their monuments and their history, famous for their arts and crafts. Both cities, furthermore, were built with what we now call town planning in mind: they are neat and orderly and easy for the visitor to find his way in—statements that are hardly true of either Tokyo or Bangkok. I may add that both Kyoto and Chiangmai are famous for the beauty of their women— justifiably so, it seemed to me.

A few miles outside the city are the famous Chiangmai craft villages, where some of Thailand's ablest artisans are at work. The villages are particularly well known for their beautiful inlaid silver bowls, paper umbrellas, teak carvings, lacquer ware, and celadon pottery.

It was in the northwest corner of what is now Thailand that the first frontiersmen who had made their way down from China about a thousand years ago settled and built their cities—of which the first was probably Fang, founded in 857 near the present northern border. Around the same time, it is conjectured, another Thai city was established at Sao, the present Luang Prabang. Somewhat later, another city grew up near the town now called Sawankalok, and in 1096 a city was built in Phayao.*

During these centuries, this northwest pocket, "the cradle of Thai culture," as it has been called, was part of the still vast but declining Cambodian empire. It is not surprising, therefore, that the incoming Thais found themselves in conflict with the land's Khmer rulers. The first major clash between the two peoples occurred in 1238, when the Cambodians dispatched an army to the north to deal with the growing Thai menace. The army was defeated, and the Thais captured Sukhothai, then the northern capital of the Cambodian empire. This was the beginning of Thai-Cambodian hostility, which has continued up to the present day, and it was the beginning also of the powerful, but short-lived, Thai state of Sukhothai, which for a time was to control an area roughly equivalent to present-day Thailand.

In part because of Burmese invasions, the Cambodian empire was on the wane, while Thai strength kept increasing during those centuries as more and more immigrants came down from the north, particularly after Kublai Khan's invasion of southern China in 1254. Some forty years after the victory at Sukhothai, the most celebrated of Sukhothai monarchs, King Ramkamheng, came to the throne, and it was during his reign, which lasted from about 1275 to 1317,

*These statements are taken from W. A. R. Wood, *History of Siam* (Bangkok: 1924); unfortunately, little is known of this first period of Thai history.

that the struggling little city-state of Sukhothai became a powerful kingdom, to which distant cities paid tribute.

But Ramkamheng was not merely a warrior. He formulated an alphabet that is essentially the same as the one used in Thailand today, and he was the author of the famous inscription on stone of which a small part has already been quoted. Further, at a time and a place when most monarchs were more interested in conquest than in justice, King Ramkamheng caused a bell to be cast and hung at Sukhothai which anyone was at liberty to ring who felt he had suffered an injustice and who desired to appeal to the monarch for judgment.

It would be an exaggeration, however, to think that the Thais took their country by conquest. For the most part it was a sparsely populated, undercultivated land on which they settled; and conflicts with the Cambodians were to a large extent rebellions of established settlers against imperialistic control. To quote Wood again: "We must not picture to ourselves the Thais as an invading army, marching southwards, attacking the Cambodian Empire, and filching away its dominions. No; the establishment of the free Thai kingdoms in Siam was the result rather of a series of rebellions than an invasion."

The present-day visitor to Bangkok may gain some idea of what life may have been like in the heyday of the Sukhothai kingdom by frequenting the resturant that attempts to revoke that particular period in Thai history. The decor recalls Sukhothai painting and carving, and there is classical dancing to traditional music. Visitors recline on cushions at low tables—though they are not required to use their fingers to eat with, as people did in older days. Leaning comfortably back and sampling the variety of delicately spiced foods

I had the feeling that the Sukhothai era, with its flourishing arts and its sumptous court life, was probably not too dissimilar from the Heian period of Japanese culture.

The great kingdom of Sukhothai endured for only 135 years; none of Ramkamheng's successors was powerful enough to keep possession of the conquests he had made. Moreover, as the kingdom of Sukhothai waned, a rival power, the city-state of Utong, which lay nearly four hundred miles to the south, waxed strong. The prince of Utong conquered many Sukhothai possessions and even parts of the Cambodian empire that Ramkamheng had never attempted. After 1350, when the Prince of Utong founded a new city at Ayudhya and proclaimed himself king, Sukhothai power dwindled to the point where its king was no more than a vassal of the king of Ayudhya. The kingdom of Ayudhya was destined to last for over four centuries, until the city was taken by the Burmese in 1767 after a siege of two years.

※　　　※

This northern region of Thailand, which saw the birth of Siamese culture, is notable for its great teak forests and for the elephants that work them. No hauling machine yet invented can rival the elephant in this field, particularly when it comes to loading logs or carting them to the river to be transported down. I was told, to my surprise, that an elephant can pull a log weighing over two tons and that two elephants in harness can pull up to five tons. They are used, also, to fell a tree at the desired angle by merely pushing against it.

Thus there is no present danger that the elephant will find himself without a job in northern Thailand. Nevertheless, his number has decreased sharply since the end of the last century, when it was estimated that there were some two hundred thousand elephants at work in the forests. Today the estimate would probably be less than half that figure.

His status in the Thai world has also fallen during the last hundred years, for in the past he was not only a beast of burden but also a piece of vital military equipment, serving a function roughly similar to that of the tank in modern warfare. "In ancient times," writes Richard Carrington, "the strength of an eastern potentate was largely measured by the number of war elephants he could put to field. The animals were heavily armored with metal plates on their heads and sides; swords were tied to their trunks and poisoned daggers to their tusks. Their riders were protected by armor or chain mail and fought with swords and javelins like knights at a medieval tournament."*

On occasions the two leaders of the opposing armies would fight a single combat on elephant-back to determine the battle's outcome. The last known joust of this kind occurred in 1592 on Thai soil between King Naresuan and the Crown Prince of Burma. Of it Prince Chula writes:

In this type of personal combat the trained beasts charged one another like the horses of European knights. The rider must hook the elephant at the right time so that its tusks would catch the opponent's elephant and lift him up so that the other rider would be exposed and unable to use his weapon. On this memorable occasion the Burmese timed his hooking splendidly which made Naresuan appear helpless. As the Crown Prince swept with his sabre attached to the long pole, the Black Prince (Naresuan) ducked and only the brim of his leather hat was cut

*Richard Carrington, *Elephants* (London: Basic Books, 1959).

off in the shape of a crescent moon. After the two elephants disengaged, they charged one another again and this time it was the Thai animal which got in below, and the hapless Crown Prince was cut in half from the shoulder to the waist.*

The Burmese army duly admitted defeat and retired from the field.

Nowhere in the world has that freak of the family, the white elephant, been treated with so much reverence, and even awe, as in Thailand, although all nations of Southeast Asia regard them as symbols of divine good fortune and on occasion have gone so far as to wage wars for possession of them. In Thailand in the past they received the same respect as members of the nobility and were given equivalent ranks, one elephant attaining the highest of all Siamese titles, Chao Phya. They ate their meals of grass and water out of large golden salvers and had personal attendants to fan them in the heat or to shade them with large umbrellas when they decided to go for a walk. Even today all white elephants automatically become royal possessions: they are presented to the king and are lodged within the palace compound. Although the white elephant no longer appears on the Thai flag, the Order of the White Elephant is still conferred for distinguished service to the country.

Indefatigable King Mongut wrote a treatise on white—or, more accurately, albino—elephants, in which he described their particular points of beauty, such as yellow eyes, white hair, white nails, pink skin, and a harmonious snore. But it is the color, the king pointed out, that finally determines the elephant's rank, highest rank going to the beast whose color is pale gold, second highest to

---

*Prince Chula Chakrabongse, *Lords of Life* (London: Alvin Redman, 1960).

the one whose skin is the color of a faded lotus petal, and third to the animal the color of a dried banana leaf. The liberal-minded monarch concluded, however, that in judging the beauty of a white elephant, as in judging that of a woman, every man is entitled to his own prejudices.

The vital role that the elephant once played in Thai life is vividly demonstrated every November at the roundup at Surin. Once simply a businesslike roundup of wild elephants in the region, it is now accompanied by spectacular displays (intended mainly for tourists), in which as many as two hundred elephants participate, accompanied of course by their mahout. (*Mahout* comes from a Hindi word meaning "elephant-driver.") The visitor is shown how the elephant is hunted and finally caught by a lasso thrown over a hind leg; elephant races, reenactments of famous elephant battles, and such lighthearted entertainment as a tug-of-war between men and elephants give the visitor as spectacular an elephant show as may be seen anywhere in the world.

Beyond the teak forests of the north dwell the relatively un-studied, "unanthropologized" hill tribes of Thailand who make their living out of the cultivation and sale of opium. They were there before present nations came into existence, and they tend to ignore present national boundaries. They do not consider themselves to be Thai any more than their fellow tribesmen in Burma or China feel that they are Burmese or Chinese. No matter where he happens to live, a Meo is a Meo, an Akha is an Akha, a Karen is a Karen.

Estimates of the hill tribe population now living in Thailand vary from about two hundred thousand to half a million—but no accurate number can possibly be given, not only because tribesmen ignore frontiers but also because many settlements are wholly unknown to government officials in Bangkok. Many tribesmen have never even seen a Thai, and of course the number that have seen a white man are very few indeed. Estimates made in 1965 of the six main tribes yield the following figures: seventy-five thousand Karen, fifty thousand Meo, twenty-eight thousand Akha, nineteen thousand Lisa, seventeen thousand Laku or Musor, and twelve thousand Yao. There are also numerous smaller groups and sub-groups, making a total of about twenty separate ethnic groups in

the whole of Thailand. However accurate or inaccurate the estimates given above may be, the figures have certainly increased since
1965 because many tribesmen have crossed over the border into
Thailand from Burma and Laos in order to escape conscription into
military service. In Thailand, they find, restrictions are few, neces-
sary contacts with officialdom are rare, and soil resources have not
been exhausted.

I visited a Meo village not very far north of Chiangmai. Relatively
close to civilization, these tribesmen are more or less accustomed
to foreign visitors—a fact that quickly became apparent when I
discovered that the villagers expected a tip for letting me take pictures of them. It was, nonetheless, a typical Meo village, consisting
of some twenty thatched wooden houses spread out over a hill-
side clearing. Much of the nearby jungle has been cut or burned away
to allow cultivation of such crops as corn, maize, coffee, and rice.
Beyond the cleared area, the jungle grew thick and lush—and I
saw how easy it would be to plant small poppy fields behind that
exuberant screen and never be found out by the authorities. (Cultivation and sale of opium are now illegal in Thailand.)

As I entered the village I was astonished by the contrast between
the rather primitive housing arrangments and the splendor of the
villagers' costume. They all seemed to be in fancy dress, and for
a moment my mind leapt back to Swiss and Austrian mountain-
dwellers. The silver neckbands, I learned later, are made from
melted-down Indian rupees that are smuggled over the mountains
through Burma. My first contact was with a short, thin man wearing
a typical Meo skullcap and carrying a primitive crossbow. Speak-
ing extremely broken English, he offered to be my guide for a fee
of ten *baht* (fifty cents). Though I hardly expected to gain much

from a conducted tour, I agreed—and when the tour was over, I had no doubts that I had got my ten-*baht*'s worth.

The village, it seemed to me, was probably wealthier than most tribal villages, for I saw a large number of domesticated animals—chickens and ducks, goats and pigs, and even ponies. The village even had a system of bamboo gutters to channel water from a mountain stream to every hut, but like all Meos the villagers made little use of the water for purposes of washing—out of fear of washing away good spirits.

In one of the huts that my guide took me to, I saw women weaving a thick and very beautiful cloth; I should have liked to buy some of it, but the price they asked seemed much too high. When I asked about a particularly well-constructed building, in front of which stood a white flagpole, my guide replied, "King's school." "Why king's school?" I asked. "King come here," was the reply "King make school." As the Chiangmai palace is not far from the village, I assumed that His Majesty had come there to dedicate the school; and I think my guess was probably right, for the guide went on, "Here king's Meo."

Most villages lack schools, and most tribesmen speak only their own language, which, generally, is an unwritten one. The Meos say that they had books once but ate them at a time of famine. This legend, as Gordon Young points out, not only explains away the Meos' illiteracy but at the same time enables them to be proud of it: they do not have to read books because they already have the knowledge inside them.*

The other large house in the village, my guide told me, belonged to the headman. "Headman have three wives," he said. "And you,"

*Gordon Young, *Hill Tribes of Northern Thailand* (Bangkok: 1962)

THAILAND ✳

I asked, "how many wives have you?" "Have no money, have no wife," was his unromantic reply, suggesting that in Meo society, as in many others, sexual rewards are in direct proportion to size of income. A Meo obtains a bride by making a payment of silver to the girl's family, the average price being the equivalent of about a hundred and fifty dollars. In most cases, the girl's consent is obtained first, and few marriages end in divorce, for if the wife leaves the husband without good cause her family is obliged to return the marriage money, while if the husband leaves his wife he loses his "deposit."

Marriage customs vary, of course, from tribe to tribe. Among the Akha, for instance, there is an annual ceremony at which a man especially appointed for the purpose deflowers young virgins in preparation for their marriage. To quote Gordon Young again: "Very little value is placed on Akha girls. . . . Women are beaten mercilessly for the slightest offence against men, and are sometimes clubbed to death."

Outside one hut I saw an old man smoking from a large bamboo water pipe. "Smoke *ganja*," my guide instructed me. *Ganja*, or marijuana, is easy to buy in Thailand and is commonly smoked; so far as I could see, it does no more harm than alcohol—and perhaps less. A less harmless drug that is also used in the village is, of course, the opium that the villagers cultivate. Although only a relatively small number of Meos (about ten percent is the estimate) are addicts, many more are occasional smokers, often using the drug as a painkiller, since medicines are scarce.

I was taken into a small, dark, windowless hut, whose only light came from the opened door and from cracks in the planked wooden walls. After my eyes had become adjusted to the dimness,

I made out a hearth in one corner, with an iron kettle, some large water jars, some flat wicker trays for winnowing rice, a stone rice grinder, and skins and clothes hanging from the wooden beams of the ceiling. On one wall was pinned a photograph of the present Mrs. Aristotle Onassis, taken from an old copy of *Life*—a gift, perhaps, from a previous visitor.

At the far end of the room, on a slightly raised wooden platform covered with cardboard, lay an old woman. She held a short pipe whose bowl was pierced by a small hole. As I watched, she carefully put a little lump of toffeelike stuff over the hole, then held the pipe above an oil lamp, and when the toffee began to melt drew a deep breath. Her cheeks pulled into her face, as she took three or four good puffs; her eyes gleamed brightly; then she lay back, resting her head on a pillow, savoring the delights of the opium. Soon she decided to have another pipe, and as she seemed unperturbed by the presence of visitors, I thought I would try to get a picture of her in spite of the dim light. I opened the lens to its widest aperture, set the shutter at half a second, and held the camera as steadily as I could. Plate 90 gives the lucky result.

My guide told me that he did not smoke himself but suggested I try it, and assured me that if I did I would "walk good." Though I was unsure what he meant, I smoked a pipe out of curiosity, but I did not take enough to walk good because I was afraid that if I did, I would walk right off and leave my cameras behind.

I was surprised to learn that the cultivation of the opium poppy is not particularly lucrative for the tribesmen (and is very hard work), but it does have the advantage of permitting them to sell their produce right in their own village. Profits are high for the traders who go traveling about the villages, buying the opium cheaply and then selling it at a high price in ports where it is smuggled out of the country (and for the smugglers themselves too, of course, as well as for officials who take bribes to look the other way, and the "pushers" in the big cities of the West). Tribesmen can make as much money, strangely enough, out of cultivating red peppers, but in order to sell the chilies they must leave their own familiar hills —a thing they do not like to do.

Until quite recently they have been left pretty much alone by the government, but lately they have got involved in two aspects of Thai politics. One is the fact that the hills have been the scene of bitter fighting between Thai troops and what are thought to have been communist-inspired rebels. And the other is the increasing international pressure being put on the government to end the cultivation of the opium poppy. Stamping it out is difficult, not only because many of the tribal settlements are difficult to reach but also because opium is their age-old means of livelihood. Other crops, in their opinion, are too speculative. There is the further consideration that the mountains in north Thailand are only the southern fringe of a large opium-growing area; probably much of the opium that finds its way into Thailand is grown in Laos, Burma, and China. It is to the credit of the Thai government that despite these difficulties opium cultivation in the country is declining.

But much needs to be done for these northern tribes. They need schools and hospitals. They need to be taught modern methods of agriculture, so that they will be able to remain in one place. Many hill tribes practice a primitive form of slash-and-burn agriculture, clearing a forest area and cultivating it intensively until the soil is barren, then moving on. In this way large forest areas are being destroyed and the land despoiled. With a rapidly increasing population and dwindling reserves of timber, Thailand can no longer afford such wasteful extravagance.

Further, the country is in danger of losing its rich and varied wild life, for deforestation means loss of living quarters for the nation's wild elephants and buffaloes, its tigers and rhinoceroses, its rare species of deer, birds, and monkeys. Many are in serious danger of extinction, while hunters and exporters of animals and animal products do nothing to make the picture any brighter.

The tribespeople, meanwhile, under increasing pressure to change their old ways, occasionally find expression for their discontent in rebellion. Military security in tribal areas has been stepped up, and at the same time welfare programs for the tribes are being implemented. The government can no longer afford to ignore their needs, nor can the tribes expect to remain in isolation. It will be unfortunate if, in the process of entering the twentieth century, they lose the valuable traditions that have given them their identity and their independence; it is to be hoped, therefore, that a way can be found to ameliorate their lot while at the same time permitting them to live out their lives on the land that they have chosen.

Perhaps even more urgent than the problems facing the hill tribes are those of the northeast, the broad ear on Thailand's elephantoid map. The northeast is the dust bowl of the country, a barren region whose poverty-stricken people are in desperate need of many things, perhaps the most urgent being more water and more roads. Able to harvest but one rice crop a year, the region's ten million inhabitants are the poorest in the country, and many of their villages, in that dusty wilderness, are completely isolated from the rest of the country, cut off by the absence of roads.

In addition, the northeast is the powder keg of Thailand, waiting uneasily for the flame that will touch off the explosion. In 1964, when Peking announced that Thailand was to be the next target for revolution and subversion in Southeast Asia, the Chinese knew very well that the northeast was the best place to begin. Since that ominous announcement, the region has been the focal point for insurgency and terrorism. Communist agents cross the Mekong River from Laos, or come down from Yunnan Province in China; they visit the remote villages, pointing out to the villagers their urgent needs and asking what the government is doing to help.

The answer, unfortunately, is not much. Welfare and development programs have been slow in getting started in these arid wastelands. Officials are often poorly trained and uninterested in the problems of the people they have been sent to help. As a result, they receive no respect from the villagers, who claim that the officials are there only to collect their salaries. When an electric generator was installed in one isolated town, it was never used because the people were too poor to buy the power it generated, not to speak of such hopelessly expensive gadgets as electric sewing machines. The people had asked for water and for roads—and the government had given them instead a useless piece of machinery. The Communist agents who have infiltrated the region, on the other hand, are free to make all sorts of glowing promises: promises cost nothing. What's more, many of the northeastern villagers are of Laotian origin, and the Laotian agents speak to them in their own dialects. Like missionaries chanting the gospel, wandering minstrels sing songs with ideological messages.

The Thai government has recently been trying to counter this missionary fervor by another: they have been encouraging country monks, who are respected by the villagers, to join the welfare battle. "To combat twentieth-century Communism," in the words of Jerrold Schecter, "Thailand has returned to third century B.C. Buddhism."* Under training programs sponsored by the government, Buddhist monks are now learning to make water jars and to dig wells, at the same time that they are being educated in public health and sanitation as well as the principles of citizenship.

But many monks object to this political involvement. They maintain that the sole duties of a monk are to follow and to teach the precepts of the Lord Buddha, and they are annoyed with the Thai government because it has forbidden them to attend Buddhist conferences in mainland China. Some believe that the use of Buddhism to counter Communism only intensifies the conflict between what they see as two ideals that are in many respects compatible.

As vital as his trunk to the elephant is the southern peninsular area to the Thai economy. The south of Thailand is one of the richest regions in the country and contributes substantially to the national income. Tin, Thailand's chief mineral resource, is mined largely in the south, especially on the island of Phuket and nearby areas, where much of it is produced by offshore dredging. Rubber, second only to rice in the Thai economy, is also found in the south.

At the beginning of the last century, most of the peninsula, including much of what is now Malaysia, consisted of a group of semiautonomous Muslim states that sent nominal tribute to Bangkok. Rivalry between Britain and Siam over the states ended at

*Jerrold Schecter, *The New Face of Buddha* (New York: Coward-McCann, 1967).

the beginning of the present century, when an agreement was made assigning some of the states to Malaya and others to Siam. The dividing line that was established then still marks the present border.

Britain and Siam both found the agreement satisfactory, but the Muslims themselves were understandably displeased at the division. Since then, Thailand's three million Mohammedans, almost all of whom live in the southern area, have expressed resentment at control by Bangkok; and there has been considerable, though unsuccessful, political activity aimed at creating a separate Muslim state in the area. The problem has been aggravated by the incursion into Thailand of Malaysian Communist guerrillas driven out of their own country. These have joined with gangs of Muslim bandits to form a hard core of terrorists who live in the dense jungles but operate on the main highways and in the cities. The two countries —Thailand and Malaysia—have now set up a headquarters at Songkhla for combined operations against terrorist activities.

Despite these problems the overall picture of peninsular Thailand is on the whole a happy one. Towns are prospering and modernizing, while in the country regional development programs are providing better medical care, roads, and education—though the standard of living is still extremely low. Southern Thailand also boasts some of the most beautiful beaches in the country, beautiful and still quite unspoiled—for it will probably be many years before they are "discovered" by the tourist.

On the line from the mouth to the eye of the cartographical

elephant of Thailand lie the ruins of the old city of Ayudhya, which was once one of the most important cities of Asia. An early traveler described it as "a city of all different peoples and the commercial center of the universe where all languages are spoken." Today, stumbling about the ruins, one wonders what it could have been like in its heyday. By all accounts, it was a splendid city of elegant canals, magnificent palaces, and hundreds of beautiful wats, one of which is said to have enshrined an image of the Buddha forty-eight feet high and covered with eight hundred pounds of gold.

It was in Ayudhya that the first contacts between Siam and the West were made. The earliest visitors were Portuguese traders and missionaries, who were soon followed by the Dutch and then the British. The latter came in the sailing ship *Globe* and brought a letter from King James I to the King of Siam. Another royal letter was brought by the first French embassy in 1624. According to Prince Chula, the letter King Louis XIV sent to King Narai "was laid on a golden salver, deposited first in a gilded royal barge propelled by sixty oarsmen in scarlet, then placed on a golden palanquin carried by ten men, also garbed in red." Surely the spectacle of so much gold and scarlet must have impressed even the ambassador of the Sun King himself.

But Europe, apparently, did not have a similar effect on the first Siamese embassy that went to Paris around the same time. They are said to have yawned at the opera, to have refused to kneel at Notre Dame during mass, and to have expressed their boredom at all the sightseeing and parties they were subjected to. If true, the Thais have learnt, since those early days, the value of diplomacy and have made good use of it in maintaining their independence. King Chulalongkorn, was very popular with the royal courts of Europe.

THAILAND

One of the most unusual Europeans ever to set foot in Asia was the Greek adventurer, Constantine Phaulkon, who, once he reached Ayudhya, decided to give up his career as a sailor and ended up the most powerful man in Siam, chief minister to King Narai. He became first a minor official at the court, where his proficiency at languages, his knowledge of Western science, and his skill at playing politics earned him one advancement after another. The ruins of his palace, just outside Ayudhya, attest to the vast sums of money he must have amassed while at the court. His life ended tragically: in the course of his career he had made powerful enemies who finally succeeded in having him arrested, tortured, and beheaded.

His wife, incidentally, was Japanese—a descendant of Japanese guards in the service of the kings of Siam. In 1628, the guards revolted against their royal master, and as a result were expelled from the country, an event that marked the end of Japanese influence in Siam for over three hundred years.

Ayudhya's downfall came in 1767, when the Burmese, after a two years' siege, finally broke through the city walls. The inevitable looting and burning that followed resulted in the loss of countless treasures of art and historical documents. All that is left of old Ayudhya today are crumbling walls and pagodas, the sad, shattered skeleton of what was once a great, bustling, glittering city.

✳   ✳

At the mouth of the Thai elephant rises the capital, which we call Bangkok but which is known to the Thais as Krung Thep, or City of Angels. Only about ten percent of the population of the country live in the capital, and most Thais have never even seen it. How bewildered a man from one of the more remote areas would feel at his first sight of the tall office buildings and hotels, the congested streets, the swimming pools! Even if he could afford it, he would be quite unable to reserve a hotel room or shop at a supermarket or—for that matter—make a telephone call. And the poverty-stricken village world that is so familiar to him would be equally bewildering and overwhelming to the city-dweller.

The advance of modern civilization often destroys much of what was valuable in the old—but it can also bring education, health, cleanliness, opportunity. The challenge that faces an emerging nation is to make the best of both worlds: to keep out the carpet-bagger and bring in the irrigation canals and the generators; to blend the traditional with the modern (as in the new Chiangmai University, for instance); to absorb new values without rejecting the old and still meaningful ones; to move into the future without losing the perspective granted by the past. I am hopful that Thailand will manage this difficult juggling trick: I should not like to see her villagers deprived of the benefits of modern civilization, but at the same time I should hate to see them lose the old-fashioned qualities that made me admire them so deeply and feel so much at home among them.

I left the City of Angels as I had entered it eighteen months before —on a ship of the Messagerie Maritime line. Saying goodbye to friends at the dock, I knew that I would be back; it is not within the human character to feel that you are leaving forever a place you have loved so well.

And I did come back. It was nearly two years later, in June of 1969, and it was then I took many of the photographs reproduced in this book. I saw many great changes in Bangkok, of course, and not all of them were improvements. Prices had gone up, there as everywhere; more canals had been filled in to make way for streets and roads, and lining them were more tall, new buildings. In the two years that I was away, elections had been held for the first time in a decade, and the Thai government was anticipating an American withdrawal from Asia. The city, in those two years, seemed to have grown more international, more like other prosperous cities of the world—and yet much was still the same. The people, the food, the festivals, the climate, the country itself—all were still there to welcome me and make me feel at home again.

They will be there when I go back next time. I am counting on it.

76. *Long, artificial finger-nails:* a typical adjunct of North Thailand dancer; the headband is jasmine.

77. *Doi Suthep monastery* near Chiangmai, the country's second largest city, is one of the most important in northern Thailand; a major relic of the Buddha is said to be buried in the courtyard.

78. *Buddha* smiles down at abbot and worshipers; portrait of the king hangs nearby.

79. *Murals* from monastery courtyard depict scenes from the life of the Buddha.

80. *Elderly monk* climbs steps to Doi Suthep, holding umbrella against the sun; balustrade behind is in the form of a serpent.

81. *Swimming pool* is a canal, and diving board is a flame tree; boys are from Chiangmai.

82. *Walls* of Chiangmai have witnessed many a bloody battle since the city's foundation seven centuries ago.

83. *Two* of Chiangmai's attractions—handicrafts, and beautiful girls; these are working in a nearby village that specializes in paper umbrellas.

84—85. *Khmer ruins* are a reminder that much of present-day Thailand was once part of the Cambodian Empire; these monuments at Pimai are strikingly similar to those of Angkor.

86. *Main street* of a ▶ village near Pimai.

87. *Hill tribes* of North Thailand inhabit their own remote mountain world; many live by cultivating the opium poppy.

89. *Silver neckbands* and head decora-▶ tions (made from smuggled Indian rupees) are a Meo status symbol.

88. *Cotton-weaving* contributes to the family income; a Meo man may have three or four wives—if he can afford them.

90. *Opium addicts* number only about ten percent of Meo population, though far more are occasional smokers.

91. *Meo man* pays about $150 for each wife.

92. *Bamboo water pipe* for smoking marijuana.

93. *Isolation* of hill tribes is ancient —but the present century seems likely to effect some profound changes in the old way of life.

◀94. *Ayudhya,* the ancient capital of Siam, was sacked and burned by the Burmese in 1767 after a two years' siege.

95. "*The commercial center* of the universe" was how one early traveler described Ayudhya; this is how it looks today.

THIS BEAUTIFUL WORLD